diabetic
AIR FRYER

pil

Publications International, Ltd.

Photograph on cover and page 75 © shutterstock.com

Pictured on the front cover: Garlic Chicken with Roasted Vegetables (*page 74*).

Pictured on the back cover (*clockwise from top left*): Buffalo Cauliflower Bites (*page 128*), Caprese Portobellos (*page 136*), and Easy Air-Fried Chicken Thighs (*page 100*).

ISBN: 978-1-64558-166-6

Manufactured in China.

8 7 6 5 4 3 2 1

Microwave Cooking: Microwave ovens vary in wattage. Use the cooking times as guidelines and check for doneness before adding more time.

Let's get social!

 @Publications_International

 @PublicationsInternational

www.pilbooks.com

TABLE OF CONTENTS

INTRODUCTION

There's no doubt that millions of people today may have diabetes or are at risk for getting diabetes. And, as such, individuals diagnosed may assume they need to follow a special restrictive diet.

Managing diabetes is key to controlling it. Eating properly, monitoring glucose levels, and managing medications are important, along with staying active, living a healthy lifestyle, and taking charge of self-care.

Many times, being overweight—especially having too much fat in the abdominal area—hampers diabetes control. For people with diabetes, the best path to weight loss is the same one that leads to getting well and staying well. There's no denying that weight loss is beneficial for people especially with type 2 diabetes who are overweight. Even a weight loss of just 5 to 10 percent of total body weight can bring impressive improvements to health. Studies show that when a person who has recently been diagnosed with diabetes loses weight, blood glucose levels drop, blood pressure improves, and cholesterol levels return to a healthier range. Medications may be decreased or even stopped altogether.

Weight loss is never easy, but finding new ways to cut calories is motivating for even the most difficult situations. The air fryer possibly can help. Cooking food in an air fryer allows individuals to use less oil and fat than traditional deep fryers, while helping to maintain the taste and texture of common comforting "fried" foods that are hard to resist. Not only is the air fryer a great substitute for these "fried" foods, it's a great appliance for cooking all types of foods. Plus, because an air fryer cooks faster, it's easier to prepare meats, chicken, fish, vegetables, and more quickly with less added fat and improved nutrient retention.

Cooking with an air fryer can be a useful and alternative method for satisfying taste and pleasurable eating. But as a diabetic, it's important to make sure the foods you prepare are part of your scheduled meal plan. Individuals with diabetes still need to monitor carbohydrates, cholesterol, sodium, and other nutrients to make sure the food consumed fits into individual diets. Anyone managing diabetes should surround themselves with knowledgeable, trustworthy, and expert advisors—the diabetes care team—who can help get information, advice, treatments, and support needed to manage diabetes effectively. This team should include a doctor and a registered dietitian nutritionist to help choose what, how much, and when to eat; help become more physically active; assist with medication; check blood glucose; and teach all they can about diabetes. And, they can possibly provide insight and ideas on how to use the air fryer most effectively with the foods in specific dietary plans.

You're on Your Way

Once you feel comfortable with your meal and activity plan, checking your blood sugar, and managing your medication, you'll be able to enjoy the great taste of food without worry. Take time to understand the workings of your air fryer and enjoy all the great foods you can prepare in it.

Helpful Hints for Using Your Air Fryer

• Read your air fryer's manufacturer's directions carefully before cooking to make sure you understand the specific features of your air fryer before starting to cook.

• Preheat your air fryer for 2 to 3 minutes before cooking.

• You can cook foods typically cooked in the oven in your air fryer. But because the air fryer is more condensed than a regular oven, it is recommended that recipes cut 25°F to 50°F off temperature and 20% off the typical cooking times.

• Avoid having foods stick to your air fryer basket by using nonstick cooking spray or cooking on parchment paper or foil. You can also get food to brown and crisp more easily by spraying occasionally with nonstick cooking spray during the cooking process.

• Don't overfill your basket. Each air fryer differs in its basket size. Cook foods in batches as needed.

• Use toothpicks to hold food in place. You may notice that light foods may blow around from the pressure of the fan. Just be sure to secure foods in the basket to prevent this. Also, place food on top of parchment paper and foil to weigh it down, so it doesn't blow around while cooking.

• Check foods while cooking by opening the air fryer basket. This will not disturb cooking times.

Once you return the basket, the cooking resumes.

• Experiment with cooking times of various foods. Test foods for doneness before consuming—check meats and poultry with a meat thermometer, and use a toothpick to test muffins and small cakes.

Estimated Cooking Temperatures/Times*

Food	Temperature	Timing
Vegetables (asparagus, broccoli, corn-on-the-cob, green beans, mushrooms, cherry tomatoes)	390°F	5 to 6 min.
Vegetables (bell peppers, cauliflower, eggplant, onions, potatoes, zucchini)	390°F	8 to 12 min.
Chicken (bone-in)	370°F	20 to 25 min.
Chicken (boneless)	370°F	12 to 15 min.
Beef (ground beef)	370°F	15 to 17 min.
Beef (steaks, roasts)	390°F	10 to 15 min.
Pork	370°F	12 to 15 min.
Fish	390°F	10 to 12 min.
Frozen Foods	390°F	10 to 15 min.

*This is just a guide. All food varies in size, weight, and texture. Be sure to test your food for preferred doneness before consuming it. Also, some foods will need to be shaken or flipped to help distribute ingredients for proper cooking.

chapter 1

WHOLESOME BREAKFASTS

Breakfast Pepperoni Flatbread

MAKES 2 SERVINGS

1 flatbread

½ cup (2 ounces) shredded mozzarella cheese

1 plum tomato, diced

12 slices turkey pepperoni, cut into quarters

1 teaspoon grated Parmesan cheese

¼ cup chopped fresh basil

1. Preheat air fryer to 370°F.

2. Place flatbread on parchment paper. Sprinkle with mozzarella cheese, tomatoes, pepperoni and Parmesan cheese.

3. Cook 3 to 5 minutes or until cheese is melted. Sprinkle with basil. Cool slightly before cutting.

Calories 170, **Total Fat** 8g, **Saturated Fat** 4g, **Cholesterol** 35mg, **Sodium** 560mg, **Carbohydrates** 10g, **Dietary Fiber** 0g, **Protein** 15g
DIETARY EXCHANGES: ½ Bread/Starch, 1½ Meat, ½ Vegetable, 1 Fat

Air-Fried Omelet Scramble

MAKES 2 SERVINGS

2 large eggs

2 tablespoons milk

¼ teaspoon salt

⅛ teaspoon black pepper

2 tablespoons chopped red and/or green bell pepper

2 tablespoons chopped onion

¼ cup (1 ounce) shredded Cheddar cheese, divided

1. Spray one 6×3-inch baking dish or two small ramekins* with nonstick cooking spray.

2. Whisk eggs, milk, salt and black pepper in medium bowl. Add bell pepper, onion and 2 tablespoons cheese. Pour into prepared dish.

3. Preheat air fryer to 350°F. Cook 10 to 12 minutes slightly breaking up eggs after 5 minutes. Top with remaining cheese.

*Depending on the size of your air fryer, you may need to modify the size of the baking dish.

Calories 110, **Total Fat** 7g, **Saturated Fat** 3.5g, **Cholesterol** 110mg, **Sodium** 430mg, **Carbohydrates** 3g, **Dietary Fiber** 0g, **Protein** 7g
DIETARY EXCHANGES: 1 Meat, ½ Vegetable, 1 Fat

Breakfast Burritos

MAKES 4 SERVINGS

- 4 turkey breakfast sausage links
- 2 eggs
- ½ teaspoon ground cumin (optional)
- 4 (6-inch) yellow or white corn tortillas
- ¼ cup salsa

1. Preheat air fryer to 370°F. Line basket with parchment paper.

2. Cook sausages 6 to 8 minutes or until browned on the outside and cooked through, shaking occasionally during cooking. Remove sausages to plate.

3. Whisk eggs and cumin, if desired, in small bowl. Heat small skillet over medium-high heat. Cook eggs until done.

4. Place sausage link in middle of each tortilla. Spoon equal amounts of scrambled egg on top of sausage. Roll up to enclose the filling; secure with toothpicks.

5. Cook in air fryer 2 to 3 minutes or until heated through.

6. Pour salsa in small bowl. Serve with burritos.

Sweet Breakfast Tacos: Substitute four 4-inch frozen pancakes for the tortillas and ¼ cup light maple syrup for the salsa. Stack pancakes on microwavable plate. Microwave on HIGH 30 to 60 seconds or until warmed through. To assemble tacos, place pancake on flat surface. Place sausage link in middle of pancake. Spoon 2 tablespoons egg along length of sausage. Fold in half. Repeat with the remaining pancakes, sausages, and scrambled egg. Pour maple syrup into small bowl. Serve on the side for dipping or for drizzling over tacos.

Calories 130, **Total Fat** 5g, **Saturated Fat** 1.5g, **Cholesterol** 110mg, **Sodium** 310mg, **Carbohydrates** 12g, **Dietary Fiber** 0g, **Protein** 8g
DIETARY EXCHANGES: ½ Bread/Starch, 1 Meat, ½ Fat

Strawberry Cinnamon French Toast

MAKES 4 SERVINGS

1 egg

¼ cup fat-free (skim) milk

½ teaspoon vanilla

4 (1-inch-thick) diagonally-cut slices French bread (about 1 ounce each)

2 teaspoons reduced-fat margarine, softened

2 packets sugar substitute*

¼ teaspoon ground cinnamon

1 cup sliced fresh strawberries

This recipe was tested with sucralose-based sugar substitute.

1. Preheat air fryer to 370°F. Spray basket with nonstick cooking spray.

2. Beat egg, milk and vanilla in shallow dish or pie plate. Lightly dip bread slices in egg mixture, coating completely.

3. Cook in batches 8 to 10 minutes or until golden brown, turning halfway through cooking time.

4. Meanwhile, combine margarine, sugar substitute and cinnamon in small bowl; stir until well blended. Spread mixture evenly over French toast; top with strawberries.

Calories 125, **Total Fat** 3g, **Saturated Fat** 1g, **Cholesterol** 53mg, **Sodium** 220mg, **Carbohydrates** 19g, **Dietary Fiber** 2g, **Protein** 5g
DIETARY EXCHANGES: 1 Bread/Starch, ½ Fruit

Cauliflower "Hash Brown" Patties

MAKES 8 SERVINGS

4 slices bacon

1 package (about 12 ounces) cauliflower rice

½ cup finely chopped onion

½ cup finely chopped red and/or green bell pepper

1 large egg

⅓ cup all-purpose flour or almond flour

½ cup (2 ounces) shredded Cheddar cheese

1 tablespoon chopped fresh chives

1 teaspoon salt

½ teaspoon black pepper

1. Preheat air fryer to 400°F. Cook bacon 8 to 10 minutes. Remove from basket to paper towels; blot any grease from bacon. Crumble into small pieces.

2. Place cauliflower in large bowl. Add bacon, onion, bell pepper, egg, flour, cheese, chives, salt and black pepper; mix well. Shape mixture into patties; place on baking sheet. Freeze 30 minutes.

3. Preheat air fryer to 370°F. Spray basket with nonstick cooking spray. Cook 12 to 15 minutes or until browned.

Calories 90, **Total Fat** 4g, **Saturated Fat** 2g, **Cholesterol** 35mg, **Sodium** 480mg, **Carbohydrates** 8g, **Dietary Fiber** 1g, **Protein** 6g
DIETARY EXCHANGES: 1½ Bread/Starch, ½ Meat, ½ Vegetable, ½ Fat

Homemade Air-Fried Bagels

MAKES 4 SERVINGS

1 cup self-rising flour

1 cup plain nonfat Greek
   yogurt

1 large egg, beaten

  Sesame seeds, poppy
    seeds, dried onion
    flakes, everything bagel
    seasoning (optional)

  Cream cheese or butter
    (optional)

1. Combine flour and yogurt in bowl of electric stand mixer with dough hook*. Beat 2 to 3 minutes or until mixture is well combined. Place dough on lightly floured surface; knead by hand about 4 to 5 minutes or until dough is smooth and elastic. Form dough into a ball.

2. Cut into four equal portions. Roll each into a ball. Pull and stretch dough to create desired shape, inserting finger into center to create hole. Repeat with remaining dough.

3. Preheat air fryer to 330°F. Line basket with parchment paper. Place bagels on parchment; brush with egg wash. Sprinkle with desired toppings. Cook 8 to 10 minutes or until lightly browned.

4. Serve with cream cheese or butter, if desired.

Or, use heavy spatula in large bowl to combine mixture.

Calories 150, **Total Fat** 1g, **Saturated Fat** 0g, **Cholesterol** 50mg, **Sodium** 440mg, **Carbohydrates** 25g, **Dietary Fiber** 1g, **Protein** 10g
DIETARY EXCHANGES: 1½ Bread/Starch

chapter 2

PERFECT FOR LUNCH

Vegetable and Hummus Muffaletta

MAKES 8 SERVINGS

1 small eggplant, cut lengthwise into ⅛-inch slices

1 yellow squash, cut lengthwise into ⅛-inch slices

1 zucchini, cut on the diagonal into ⅛-inch slices

1 tablespoon extra virgin olive oil

¼ teaspoon salt

¼ teaspoon black pepper

1 boule or round bread (8 inches), cut in half horizontally

1 container (8 ounces) hummus, any flavor

1 jar (12 ounces) roasted red bell peppers, drained

1 jar (6 ounces) marinated artichoke hearts, drained and chopped

1 small tomato, thinly sliced

1. Combine eggplant, squash, zucchini, oil, salt and black pepper in large bowl; toss to coat.

2. Preheat air fryer to 390°F. Cook vegetables in batches 4 to 6 minutes, shaking halfway during cooking, until tender and golden. Cool to room temperature.

3. Scoop out bread from both halves of boule, leaving about 1 inch of bread on edges and about 1½ inches on bottom. (Reserve bread for bread crumbs or croutons.) Spread hummus evenly on inside bottom of bread. Layer vegetables, roasted peppers, artichokes and tomato over hummus; cover with top half of bread. Wrap stuffed loaf tightly in plastic wrap. Refrigerate at least 1 hour before cutting into wedges.

Substitution: You can substitute a red bell pepper for the jarred peppers and roast it in the air fryer. Preheat air fryer to 390°F. Cook 15 minutes, turning once or twice. Let sit in air fryer 10 minutes longer to loosen skin. Carefully remove skin with paring knife.

Calories 270, **Total Fat** 7g, **Saturated Fat** 1g, **Cholesterol** 0mg, **Sodium** 720mg, **Carbohydrates** 44g, **Dietary Fiber** 3g, **Protein** 8g
DIETARY EXCHANGES: 2 Bread/Starch, 2 Vegetable, 1 Fat

Buffalo Chicken Wraps

MAKES 2 SERVINGS

2 boneless skinless chicken breasts (about 4 ounces each)

4 tablespoons buffalo wing sauce, divided

1 cup broccoli slaw

1½ teaspoons light blue cheese salad dressing

2 (8-inch) whole wheat tortillas, warmed

1. Place chicken in large resealable food storage bag. Add 2 tablespoons buffalo sauce; seal bag. Marinate in refrigerator 15 minutes.

2. Preheat air fryer to 370°F. Cook 8 to 10 minutes per side or until no longer pink in center. When cool enough to handle, slice chicken; combine with remaining 2 tablespoons buffalo sauce in medium bowl.

3. Combine broccoli slaw and blue cheese dressing in medium bowl; mix well.

4. Arrange chicken and broccoli slaw evenly down center of each tortilla. Roll up to secure filling. To serve, cut in half diagonally.

Tip: If you do not like the spicy flavor of buffalo wing sauce, substitute your favorite barbecue sauce.

Calories 340, **Total Fat** 7g, **Saturated Fat** 1.5g, **Cholesterol** 85mg, **Sodium** 730mg, **Carbohydrates** 38g, **Dietary Fiber** 0g, **Protein** 31g
DIETARY EXCHANGES: 1½ Bread/Starch, 3½ Meat, 1 Vegetable, ½ Fat

Chicken Salad with Creamy Tarragon Dressing

MAKES 4 SERVINGS

Creamy Tarragon Dressing
(recipe follows)

1 pound boneless skinless chicken breasts

1 teaspoon Cajun or Creole seasoning*

1 package (10 ounces) mixed salad greens

2 unpeeled apples, cored and thinly sliced

1 cup packed alfalfa sprouts

2 tablespoons raisins

Adjust your seasoning if you prefer more or less of a spicier taste.

1. Prepare Creamy Tarragon Dressing. Preheat air fryer to 370°F.

2. Season chicken with Cajun seasoning. Spray chicken with nonstick cooking spray. Cook in batches 10 to 12 minutes or until no longer pink in center.

3. Divide salad greens among four large plates. Arrange chicken, apples and sprouts on top of greens. Sprinkle with raisins. Serve with dressing.

Creamy Tarragon Dressing

MAKES ABOUT 1 CUP

½ cup plain yogurt

¼ cup sour cream

¼ cup frozen apple juice concentrate

1 tablespoon spicy brown mustard

1 tablespoon minced fresh tarragon

Combine all ingredients in small bowl.

Calories 320, **Total Fat** 7g, **Saturated Fat** 3g, **Cholesterol** 95mg, **Sodium** 170mg, **Carbohydrates** 33g, **Dietary Fiber** 3g, **Protein** 31g
DIETARY EXCHANGES: 3½ Meat, 1½ Fruit, ½ Fat

Salmon-Potato Cakes with Mustard Tartar Sauce

MAKES 4 SERVINGS

3 small unpeeled red potatoes (8 ounces), halved

1 cup water

1 cup flaked cooked salmon

2 green onions, chopped

1 egg white

2 tablespoons chopped fresh parsley, divided

½ teaspoon Cajun or Creole seasoning

1 tablespoon light mayonnaise

1 tablespoon plain nonfat yogurt or fat-free sour cream

2 teaspoons coarse grain mustard

1 tablespoon chopped dill pickle

1 teaspoon lemon juice

1. Place potatoes and water in medium saucepan. Bring to a boil. Reduce heat and simmer about 15 minutes or until potatoes are tender. Drain. Mash potatoes with fork, leaving chunky texture.

2. Combine mashed potatoes, salmon, green onions, egg white, 1 tablespoon parsley and Cajun seasoning in medium bowl.

3. Preheat air fryer to 370°F. Gently shape salmon mixture into patties; flatten slightly. Cook 5 to 6 minutes, turning halfway through cooking, until browned and heated through.

4. Meanwhile, combine mayonnaise, yogurt, mustard, remaining 1 tablespoon parsley, pickle and lemon juice in small bowl. Serve sauce with cakes.

Calories 200, **Total Fat** 4.5g, **Saturated Fat** 1g, **Cholesterol** 20mg, **Sodium** 300mg, **Carbohydrates** 27g, **Dietary Fiber** 3g, **Protein** 12g
DIETARY EXCHANGES: 1½ Bread/Starch, 2 Meat, 1 Fat

Bell Pepper and Ricotta Calzones

MAKES 6 SERVINGS

2 teaspoons olive oil

1 medium red bell pepper, diced

1 medium green bell pepper, diced

1 small onion, diced

½ teaspoon Italian seasoning

⅛ teaspoon black pepper

1 clove garlic, minced

1¼ cups marinara sauce, divided

¼ cup part-skim ricotta cheese

⅛ cup part-skim mozzarella cheese

1 package (14 ounces) refrigerated pizza dough

1. Heat oil in medium nonstick skillet over medium heat. Add bell peppers, onion, Italian seasoning and black pepper. Cook about 8 minutes, stirring occasionally, until vegetables are tender. Add garlic, and cook, stirring constantly, 1 minute. Stir in ½ cup marinara sauce; cook about 2 minutes or until thickened slightly. Transfer vegetable mixture to plate; let cool slightly.

2. Combine ricotta cheese and mozzarella cheese in small bowl. Unroll pizza dough and cut into six (4×4-inch) squares. Pat each square into 5×5-inch square. Spoon ⅓ cup vegetable mixture into center of each square. Top vegetables with 1 tablespoon cheese mixture. Fold dough over filling to form triangle; pinch and fold edges together to seal.

3. Preheat air fryer to 370°F. Line basket with parchment paper.

4. Cook in batches 8 to 10 minutes or until lightly browned. Cool 5 minutes. Serve with remaining marinara sauce.

Calories 240, **Total Fat** 6g, **Saturated Fat** 1.5g, **Cholesterol** 5mg, **Sodium** 600mg, **Carbohydrates** 39g, **Dietary Fiber** 2g, **Protein** 8g
DIETARY EXCHANGES: 2½ Bread/Starch, ½ Vegetable, ½ Fat

Grilled 3-Cheese Sandwiches

MAKES 2 SANDWICHES

2 slices (1 ounce each) Muenster cheese

2 slices (1 ounce each) Swiss cheese

2 slices (1 ounce each) Cheddar cheese

4 slices sourdough bread

2 teaspoons Dijon mustard or Dijon mustard mayonnaise

2 teaspoons melted butter

1. Preheat air fryer to 370°F.

2. Place one slice of each cheese on two bread slices. Spread mustard over cheese; top with remaining bread slices. Brush outsides of sandwiches with butter.

3. Cook 3 to 5 minutes or until cheeses are melted and sandwiches are golden brown.

Calories 490, **Total Fat** 25g, **Saturated Fat** 14g, **Cholesterol** 65mg, **Sodium** 890mg, **Carbohydrates** 38g, **Dietary Fiber** 0g, **Protein** 27g
DIETARY EXCHANGES: 2½ Bread/Starch, 3 Meat, 3 Fat

Greek Chicken Burgers with Cucumber Yogurt Sauce

MAKES 4 SERVINGS

½ cup plus 2 tablespoons plain nonfat Greek yogurt

½ medium cucumber, peeled, seeded and finely chopped

Juice of ½ lemon

3 cloves garlic, minced, divided

2 teaspoons finely chopped fresh mint *or* ½ teaspoon dried mint

⅛ teaspoon salt

⅛ teaspoon ground white pepper

Burgers

1 pound ground chicken breast

3 ounces reduced-fat crumbled feta cheese

4 large kalamata olives, rinsed, patted dry and minced

1 egg

½ to 1 teaspoon dried oregano

¼ teaspoon black pepper

Mixed baby lettuce (optional)

Fresh mint leaves (optional)

1. Combine yogurt, cucumber, lemon juice, 2 cloves garlic, 2 teaspoons chopped mint, salt and white pepper in medium bowl; mix well. Cover and refrigerate until ready to serve.

2. For burgers, combine chicken, cheese, olives, egg, oregano, black pepper and remaining 1 clove garlic in large bowl; mix well. Shape mixture into four patties.

3. Preheat air fryer to 370°F. Spray basket with nonstick cooking spray. Cook 12 to 15 minutes or until cooked through (165°F).

4. Serve burgers with sauce and mixed greens, if desired. Garnish with mint leaves.

Calories 270, **Total Fat** 12g, **Saturated Fat** 4g, **Cholesterol** 110mg, **Sodium** 430mg, **Carbohydrates** 6g, **Dietary Fiber** 0g, **Protein** 31g
DIETARY EXCHANGES: 3½ Meat, ½ Vegetable, 1 Fat

Veggie Pizza Pitas

MAKES 2 SERVINGS

1 whole wheat pita bread round, cut in half horizontally (to make 2 rounds)

2 tablespoons pizza sauce

½ teaspoon dried basil

⅛ teaspoon red pepper flakes (optional)

½ cup sliced mushrooms

¼ cup thinly sliced green bell pepper

¼ cup thinly sliced red onion

½ cup (4 ounces) shredded mozzarella cheese

1 teaspoon grated Parmesan cheese

1. Arrange pita rounds, rough sides up, in single layer on parchment paper. Spread 1 tablespoon pizza sauce evenly over each round to within ¼ inch of edge. Sprinkle with basil and red pepper flakes, if desired. Top with mushrooms, bell pepper and onion. Sprinkle with mozzarella cheese.

2. Preheat air fryer to 370°F.

3. Cook 5 to 7 minutes until mozzarella cheese melts. Sprinkle ½ teaspoon Parmesan cheese over each pita round.

Calories 150, **Total Fat** 6g, **Saturated Fat** 3.5g, **Cholesterol** 20mg, **Sodium** 370mg, **Carbohydrates** 14g, **Dietary Fiber** 1g, **Protein** 10g
DIETARY EXCHANGES: ½ Bread/Starch, 1 Meat, ½ Vegetable, 1 Fat

Japanese Fried Chicken on Watercress

MAKES 4 SERVINGS

1 pound boneless skinless chicken breasts, cut into 2-inch pieces

2 tablespoons reduced-sodium soy sauce

1 tablespoon sake

3 cloves garlic, minced

1 teaspoon minced fresh ginger

¼ cup cornstarch

2 tablespoons all-purpose flour

Salad

¼ cup unseasoned rice vinegar

3 teaspoons reduced-sodium soy sauce

1 teaspoon dark sesame oil

2 bunches watercress, trimmed of tough stems

1 pint grape tomatoes, halved

1. Place chicken in large resealable food storage bag. Mix 2 tablespoons soy sauce, sake, garlic and ginger in small bowl. Pour over chicken and marinate in refrigerator at least 30 minutes, turning bag occasionally.

2. Combine cornstarch and flour in shallow dish. Drain chicken and discard marinade. Roll chicken pieces in cornstarch mixture and shake off excess.

3. Preheat air fryer to 370°F. Cook in batches 8 to 10 minutes or until chicken is golden brown.

4. For salad, whisk together vinegar, 3 teaspoons soy sauce and sesame oil in small bowl. Arrange watercress and tomatoes on serving plates. Drizzle with dressing and top with chicken.

Calories 260, **Total Fat** 4g, **Saturated Fat** 1g, **Cholesterol** 85mg, **Sodium** 620mg, **Carbohydrates** 28g, **Dietary Fiber** 2g, **Protein** 29g
DIETARY EXCHANGES: ½ Bread/Starch, 3½ Meat, 1½ Vegetable

Spinach & Roasted Pepper Panini

MAKES 6 SERVINGS

1 loaf (12 ounces) focaccia

1½ cups spinach leaves (about 12 leaves)

1 jar (about 7 ounces) roasted red peppers, drained

4 ounces fontina cheese, thinly sliced

¾ cup thinly sliced red onion

Olive oil (optional)

1. Cut focaccia in half horizontally. Layer bottom half with spinach, peppers, cheese and onion. Cover with top half of focaccia. Brush outsides of sandwich lightly with oil, if desired. Cut sandwich into six equal pieces.

2. Preheat air fryer to 370°F. Line basket with parchment paper. Cook in batches 3 to 5 minutes or until cheese melts and bread is golden brown.

Note: Focaccia can be found in the bakery section of most supermarkets. It is often available in different flavors, such as tomato, herb, cheese or onion.

Calories 220, **Total Fat** 10g, **Saturated Fat** 3g, **Cholesterol** 15mg, **Sodium** 570mg, **Carbohydrates** 23g, **Dietary Fiber** 1g, **Protein** 10g
DIETARY EXCHANGES: 1½ Bread/Starch, ½ Meat, ½ Vegetable, 1½ Fat

Portobello Mushroom Sandwich

MAKES 1 SERVING

1 large portobello mushroom, cleaned and stemmed

1 thin slice red onion

¼ medium green bell pepper, halved

1 whole wheat hamburger bun, split and lightly toasted

1 tablespoon fat-free Italian salad dressing

1 slice (1 ounce) reduced-fat part-skim mozzarella cheese (optional)

1. Preheat air fryer to 390°F.

2. Brush mushroom, onion, bell pepper and cut sides of bun with dressing; set bun aside.

3. Cook vegetables 6 to 8 minutes or until vegetables are tender.

4. Top warm mushroom with cheese, if desired. Cook 1 minute or until cheese is melted.

5. Cut pepper into strips. Place mushroom on bottom half of bun; top with onion slice and pepper strips. Cover with top half of bun.

Calories 200, **Total Fat** 3g, **Saturated Fat** 0.5g, **Cholesterol** 0mg, **Sodium** 420mg, **Carbohydrates** 35g, **Dietary Fiber** 2g, **Protein** 9g
DIETARY EXCHANGES: 1½ Bread/Starch, 1½ Vegetable

Lentil Burgers

MAKES 4 SERVINGS

1 can (about 14 ounces) vegetable broth

1 cup dried lentils, rinsed and sorted

1 small carrot, grated

¼ cup coarsely chopped mushrooms

1 egg

¼ cup plain dry bread crumbs

3 tablespoons finely chopped onion

2 to 4 cloves garlic, minced

1 teaspoon dried thyme

¼ cup plain nonfat yogurt

¼ cup chopped seeded cucumber

½ teaspoon dried mint

¼ teaspoon dried dill weed

¼ teaspoon black pepper

⅛ teaspoon salt

Dash hot pepper sauce (optional)

Kaiser rolls (optional)

1. Bring broth to a boil in medium saucepan over high heat. Stir in lentils; reduce heat to low. Simmer, covered, about 30 minutes or until lentils are tender and liquid is absorbed. Cool to room temperature.

2. Place lentils, carrot and mushrooms in food processor or blender; process until finely chopped but not smooth. (Some whole lentils should still be visible.) Stir in egg, bread crumbs, onion, garlic and thyme. Refrigerate, covered, 2 to 3 hours.

3. Shape lentil mixture into four (½-inch-thick) patties.

4. Preheat air fryer to 390°F. Spray basket with nonstick cooking spray. Cook patties in batches 8 to 10 minutes or until browned.

5. Meanwhile, for sauce, combine yogurt, cucumber, mint, dill weed, black pepper, salt and hot pepper sauce, if desired, in small bowl. Serve burgers on rolls with sauce.

Calories 240, **Total Fat** 2g, **Saturated Fat** 0.5g, **Cholesterol** 45mg, **Sodium** 210mg, **Carbohydrates** 41g, **Dietary Fiber** 7g, **Protein** 15g
DIETARY EXCHANGES: 2½ Bread/Starch, 1 Vegetable

Tasty Turkey Turnovers

MAKES 6 SERVINGS

1 package (about 8 ounces) refrigerated crescent roll sheet

2 tablespoons honey mustard, plus addtional for serving

3 ounces thinly sliced lean deli turkey breast

¾ cup packaged broccoli coleslaw mix

1 egg white, beaten

1. Roll out dough onto lightly floured surface. Using a wide glass or cookie cutter, cut into 3½-inch circles. Spread 2 tablespoons honey mustard lightly over dough circles; top with turkey and coleslaw mix. Brush edges of dough with beaten egg white. Fold circles in half; press edges with tines of fork to seal. Brush with egg white.

2. Preheat air fryer to 370°F. Spray basket with nonstick cooking spray.

3. Cook in batches 6 to 7 minutes or until golden brown. Let stand 5 minutes before serving. Serve warm or at room temperature with additional honey mustard for dipping, if desired.

Calories 160, **Total Fat** 7g, **Saturated Fat** 0g, **Cholesterol** 5mg, **Sodium** 440mg, **Carbohydrates** 19g, **Dietary Fiber** 0g, **Protein** 6g
DIETARY EXCHANGES: 1 Bread/Starch, ½ Meat, 1 Fat

Tuna Melts

MAKES 2 SERVINGS

- 1 can (about 5 ounces) chunk white tuna packed in water, drained and flaked
- ½ cup packaged coleslaw mix
- 1 tablespoon sliced green onion
- 1 tablespoon light mayonnaise
- ½ tablespoon Dijon mustard
- ¼ teaspoon dried dill weed (optional)
- 2 English muffins, split
- ¼ cup (1 ounce) shredded reduced-fat Cheddar cheese

1. Combine tuna, coleslaw mix and green onion in medium bowl. Combine mayonnaise, mustard and dill weed, if desired, in small bowl. Stir mayonnaise mixture into tuna mixture. Spread tuna mixture onto muffin halves.

2. Preheat air fryer to 370°F. Cook 3 to 4 minutes or until heated through and lightly browned. Sprinkle with cheese. Cook 1 to 2 minutes until cheese melts.

Calories 260, **Total Fat** 7g, **Saturated Fat** 5g, **Cholesterol** 40mg, **Sodium** 690mg, **Carbohydrates** 27g, **Dietary Fiber** 0g, **Protein** 22g
DIETARY EXCHANGES: 1½ Bread/Starch, 3 Meat, 1 Fat

Caprese Portobello Burgers

MAKES 4 SERVINGS

3 ounces mozzarella cheese, diced

2 plum tomatoes, chopped

2 tablespoons chopped fresh basil

1 tablespoon light balsamic vinaigrette

1 clove garlic, crushed

⅛ teaspoon black pepper

4 portobello mushrooms (about ¾ pound), gills and stems removed

4 whole wheat sandwich thin rounds, toasted

1. Preheat air fryer to 350°F. Spray basket with nonstick cooking spray. Meanwhile, combine cheese, tomatoes, basil, vinaigrette, garlic and pepper in small bowl.

2. Cook mushrooms in batches 5 to 7 minutes or until slightly tender. Spoon one fourth of tomato mixture into each cap. Cook 2 to 3 minutes or until is cheese melted. Serve on sandwich thins.

Note: Cooked portobello mushrooms can be frozen and will keep for several months. Store in plastic containers or freezer bags.

Calories 180, **Total Fat** 5g, **Saturated Fat** 2g, **Cholesterol** 15mg, **Sodium** 340mg, **Carbohydrates** 28g, **Dietary Fiber** 1g, **Protein** 12g
DIETARY EXCHANGES: 1½ Bread/Starch, 1 Meat, 1 Vegetable, ½ Fat

Salmon Croquettes

MAKES 5 SERVINGS

1 can (14¾ ounces) pink salmon, drained and flaked

½ cup mashed potatoes*

1 egg, beaten

3 tablespoons diced red bell pepper

2 tablespoons sliced green onion

1 tablespoon chopped fresh parsley

½ cup seasoned dry bread crumbs

Use mashed potatoes that are freshly made, leftover, or potatoes made from instant potatoes.

1. Combine salmon, potatoes, egg, bell pepper, green onion and parsley in medium bowl; mix well.

2. Place bread crumbs on medium plate. Shape salmon mixture into 10 croquettes about 3 inches long by 1 inch wide. Roll croquettes in crumbs to coat. Refrigerate 15 to 20 minutes or until firm.

3. Preheat air fryer to 350°F. Cook in batches 6 to 8 minutes or until browned. Serve immediately.

Calories 200, **Total Fat** 6g, **Saturated Fat** 1.5g, **Cholesterol** 110mg, **Sodium** 560mg, **Carbohydrates** 12g, **Dietary Fiber** 0g, **Protein** 24g
DIETARY EXCHANGES: 1 Bread/Starch, 3 Meat, ½ Fat

Baked Pork Buns

MAKES 10 SERVINGS

1 tablespoon oil

2 cups coarsely chopped bok choy

1 small onion or large shallot, thinly sliced

1 container (18 ounces) refrigerated shredded barbecue pork

2 packages (10 ounces each) refrigerated jumbo buttermilk biscuit dough (5 biscuits per package)

1. Heat oil in large skillet over medium-high heat. Add bok choy and onion; cook and stir 8 to 10 minutes or until vegetables are tender. Remove from heat; stir in barbecue pork.

2. Lightly flour work surface. Separate biscuits; split each biscuit in half to create two thin biscuits. Flatten each biscuit half into 5-inch circle.

3. Spoon heaping tablespoon of pork mixture onto one side of each circle. Fold dough over filling to form half circle; press edges to seal.

4. Preheat air fryer to 350°F. Line basket with parchment paper; spray with nonstick cooking spray.

5. Cook in batches 8 to 10 minutes or until golden brown.

Calories 240, **Total Fat** 8g, **Saturated Fat** 3g, **Cholesterol** 20mg, **Sodium** 860mg, **Carbohydrates** 34g, **Dietary Fiber** 0g, **Protein** 10g
DIETARY EXCHANGES: 2 Bread/Starch, 1 Meat, ½ Vegetable, 1 Fat

Spicy Eggplant Burgers

MAKES 4 SERVINGS

1 eggplant
   (about 1¼ pounds)

2 egg whites

½ cup Italian-style panko
   bread crumbs

3 tablespoons chipotle
   mayonnaise or light
   mayonnaise

4 whole wheat hamburger
   buns, warmed

1½ cups loosely packed baby
   spinach

8 thin slices tomato

4 slices pepper jack cheese

1. Cut four (½-inch-thick) slices from widest part of eggplant. Beat egg whites in shallow bowl. Place panko on medium plate.

2. Dip eggplant slices in egg whites; dredge in panko, pressing gently to adhere. Spray with nonstick cooking spray.

3. Preheat air fryer to 370°F. Line basket with foil. Cook in batches 6 to 8 minutes on each side or until golden brown.

4. Spread mayonnaise on bottom halves of buns; top with spinach, tomatoes, eggplant, cheese and tops of buns.

Calories 350, **Total Fat** 14g, **Saturated Fat** 4g, **Cholesterol** 15mg, **Sodium** 450mg, **Carbohydrates** 41g, **Dietary Fiber** 5g, **Protein** 10g
DIETARY EXCHANGES: 2 Bread/Starch, ½ Meat, 2 Vegetable, 2 Fat

chapter 3

DINNER WINNERS

Ricotta and Spinach Hasselback Chicken

MAKES 2 SERVINGS

½ cup fresh baby spinach leaves

1 teaspoon olive oil

2 tablespoons reduced-fat ricotta cheese

2 boneless skinless chicken breasts (about 4 ounces each)

⅛ teaspoon salt

⅛ teaspoon black pepper

2 tablespoons shredded reduced-fat Cheddar cheese

1. Place spinach and oil in small microwavable dish. Microwave on HIGH 20 to 30 seconds or until spinach is slightly wilted. Stir ricotta cheese into spinach; mix well.

2. Cut four diagonal slits three fourths of the way into each chicken breast (do not cut all the way through). Place about 1 teaspoon ricotta mixture into each slit. Sprinkle chicken with salt and pepper.

3. Preheat air fryer to 390°F. Line basket with foil.

4. Cook 12 minutes. Top chicken with Cheddar cheese.

5. Cook 4 to 6 minutes or until cheese melts, chicken is golden and juices run clear.

Calories 180, **Total Fat** 7g, **Saturated Fat** 3g, **Cholesterol** 65mg, **Sodium** 520mg, **Carbohydrates** 2g, **Dietary Fiber** 0g, **Protein** 26g
DIETARY EXCHANGES: ½ Meat, 1 Fat

Roast Dill Scrod with Asparagus

MAKES 4 SERVINGS

1 bunch (12 ounces) asparagus spears, ends trimmed

1 teaspoon olive oil

4 scrod or cod fillets (about 5 ounces each)

1 tablespoon lemon juice

1 teaspoon dried dill weed

½ teaspoon salt

¼ teaspoon black pepper
Paprika (optional)

1. Preheat air fryer to 390°F. Line basket with parchment paper.

2. Drizzle asparagus with oil. Roll asparagus to coat lightly with oil. Cook 8 to 10 minutes or until tender. Remove; keep warm.

3. Drizzle fish with lemon juice. Combine dill weed, salt and pepper in small bowl; sprinkle over fish.

4. Cook 10 to 12 minutes or until fish is opaque in center and begins to flake when tested with a fork. Place fish and asparagus on serving plate. Sprinkle with paprika, if desired.

Calories 150, **Total Fat** 2g, **Saturated Fat** 0g, **Cholesterol** 60mg, **Sodium** 370mg, **Carbohydrates** 4g, **Dietary Fiber** 2g, **Protein** 27g
DIETARY EXCHANGES: 3½ Meat, 1 Vegetable

Breaded Pork Cutlets with Tonkatsu Sauce

MAKES 4 SERVINGS

Tonkatsu Sauce (recipe follows)

½ cup all-purpose flour

2 eggs, beaten with 2 tablespoons water

1 cup panko bread crumbs

1 pound pork tenderloin, trimmed of fat and sliced into ½-inch-thick pieces

2 cups hot cooked rice

1. Prepare Tonkatsu Sauce; set aside.

2. Place flour in shallow dish. Place eggs in another shallow dish. Spread panko on medium plate. Dip each pork slice first in flour, then egg. Shake off excess and coat in panko.

3. Preheat air fryer to 370°F. Cook 12 to 15 minutes or until cooked through.

4. Serve over rice with Tonkatsu Sauce.

Tonkatsu Sauce

MAKES ABOUT ⅓ CUP SAUCE

¼ cup reduced-sodium ketchup

1 tablespoon reduced-sodium soy sauce

2 teaspoons sugar

2 teaspoons mirin (Japanese sweet rice wine)

1 teaspoon Worcestershire sauce

½ teaspoon grated fresh ginger

1 clove garlic, minced

Combine ketchup, soy sauce, sugar, mirin, Worcestershire sauce, ginger and garlic in small bowl.

Calories 420, **Total Fat** 5g, **Saturated Fat** 1.5g, **Cholesterol** 160mg, **Sodium** 290mg, **Carbohydrates** 57g, **Dietary Fiber** 1g, **Protein** 33g
DIETARY EXCHANGES: 3 Bread/Starch, 3 Meat

Teriyaki Salmon

MAKES 2 SERVINGS

¼ cup dark sesame oil
  Juice of 1 lemon
¼ cup soy sauce
2 tablespoons packed brown
  sugar
1 clove garlic, minced
2 salmon fillets (about
  4 ounces each)
  Hot cooked rice (optional)
  Toasted sesame seeds and
  green onions (optional)

1. Whisk oil, lemon juice, soy sauce, brown sugar and garlic in medium bowl. Place salmon in large resealable food storage bag; add marinade. Refrigerate at least 2 hours.

2. Preheat air fryer to 350°F. Spray basket with nonstick cooking spray.

3. Cook 8 to 10 minutes until salmon is crispy and easily flakes when tested with a fork. Serve with rice and garnish as desired.

Calories 320, **Total Fat** 22g, **Saturated Fat** 4.5g, **Cholesterol** 60mg, **Sodium** 650mg, **Carbohydrates** 4g, **Dietary Fiber** 0g, **Protein** 24g
DIETARY EXCHANGES: 3 Meat, 3 Fat

Beer Air-Fried Chicken

MAKES 4 SERVINGS

1⅓ cups light-colored beer,
  such as pale ale

2 tablespoons buttermilk

1¼ cups panko bread crumbs

½ cup grated Parmesan
  cheese

4 chicken breast cutlets
  (about 1¼ pounds)

½ teaspoon salt

¼ teaspoon black pepper

1. Combine beer and buttermilk in shallow dish. Combine panko and Parmesan cheese in another shallow dish.

2. Sprinkle chicken with salt and pepper. Dip in beer mixture; roll in panko mixture to coat.

3. Preheat air fryer to 370°F. Line basket with foil; spray with nonstick cooking spray.

4. Cook in batches 18 to 20 minutes or until chicken is no longer pink in center.

Tip: To make a substitution for buttermilk, place 1 teaspoon lemon juice or distilled white vinegar in a measuring cup and add enough milk to measure ⅓ cup. Stir and let the mixture stand at room temperature for 5 minutes. Discard leftover mixture.

Calories 330, **Total Fat** 6g, **Saturated Fat** 3g, **Cholesterol** 95mg, **Sodium** 670mg, **Carbohydrates** 22g, **Dietary Fiber** 0g, **Protein** 42g
DIETARY EXCHANGES: 1 Bread/Starch, 1 Meat, ½ Fat

Baked Fish with Thai Pesto

MAKES 6 SERVINGS

1 to 2 jalapeño peppers,*
   coarsely chopped

1 lemon

2 green onions, thinly sliced

1 tablespoon chopped fresh
   ginger

2 cloves garlic, minced

1 cup lightly packed fresh
   basil leaves

¾ cup lightly packed fresh
   cilantro leaves

2 tablespoons lightly packed
   fresh mint leaves

2 tablespoons unsalted
   roasted peanuts

1 tablespoon sweetened
   shredded coconut

½ teaspoon sugar

3 tablespoons peanut oil

1½ pounds boneless fish fillets
   (such as salmon, halibut,
   cod or orange roughy)

   Foil

   Lemon and cucumber slices

*Jalapeño peppers can sting and irritate
the skin, so wear rubber gloves when
handling peppers and do not touch your
eyes.*

1. Place jalapeño peppers in blender or food processor.

2. Grate peel of lemon. Juice lemon to measure 2 tablespoons. Add peel and juice to blender.

3. Add green onions, ginger, garlic, basil, cilantro, mint, peanuts, coconut and sugar to blender; blend until finely chopped. With motor running, slowly pour in oil; blend until mixed.

4. Preheat air fryer to 370°F. Rinse fish and pat dry with paper towels. Place fillets on foil. Spread solid thin layer of pesto over each fillet.

5. Cook in batches 8 to 10 minutes or until fish begins to flake when tested with a fork and is just opaque in center. Transfer fish to serving platter. Garnish with lemon and cucumber slices.

Calories 330, **Total Fat** 24g, **Saturated Fat** 5g, **Cholesterol** 60mg, **Sodium** 70mg, **Carbohydrates** 3g, **Dietary Fiber** 1g, **Protein** 25g
DIETARY EXCHANGES: 3 Meat, 3 Fat

Garlic Chicken with Roasted Vegetables

MAKES 4 SERVINGS

3 tablespoons olive oil

1 teaspoon salt

1 teaspoon dried oregano

1 teaspoon paprika

½ teaspoon black pepper

2 cloves garlic, minced

4 boneless skinless chicken breasts (about 1 pound)

2 cups Brussels sprouts, trimmed and halved

2 cups small yellow onions, cut into wedges

1 cup frozen crinkle-cut carrots

Salt and black pepper (optional)

1. Combine 2 tablespoons oil, 1 teaspoon salt, oregano, paprika, ½ teaspoon black pepper and garlic in small bowl. Brush over chicken.

2. Preheat air fryer to 370°F. Line basket with parchment paper. Cook chicken in batches 15 to 20 minutes or until chicken is browned and no longer pink in center. Remove from air fryer; keep warm.

3. Toss Brussels sprouts, onions and carrots with remaining 1 tablespoon oil in medium bowl; season with salt and pepper if desired. Increase air fryer to 390°F. Cook vegetables in batches 6 to 8 minutes or until tender and lightly browned.

Calories 220, **Total Fat** 10g, **Saturated Fat** 1.5g, **Cholesterol** 58mg, **Sodium** 350mg, **Carbohydrates** 7g, **Dietary Fiber** 1g, **Protein** 26g
DIETARY EXCHANGES: 3½ Meat, 1½ Fat

Parmesan-Crusted Tilapia

MAKES 6 SERVINGS

⅔ cup plus 2 tablespoons grated Parmesan cheese, divided

⅔ cup panko bread crumbs

⅓ cup prepared light Alfredo sauce (refrigerated or jarred)

1½ teaspoons dried parsley flakes

6 tilapia fillets (3 ounces each)

Shaved Parmesan cheese (optional)

Minced fresh parsley (optional)

1. Combine ⅔ cup grated cheese and panko in medium bowl; mix well. Combine Alfredo sauce, remaining 2 tablespoons grated cheese and parsley flakes in small bowl; mix well. Spread mixture over top of fish, coating in thick even layer. Top with panko mixture, pressing in gently to adhere.

2. Preheat air fryer to 390°F. Line basket with foil or parchment paper; spray with nonstick cooking spray.

3. Cook in batches 8 to 10 minutes or until crust is golden brown and fish begins to flake when tested with a fork. Garnish with shaved Parmesan and fresh parsley.

Calories 160, **Total Fat** 5g, **Saturated Fat** 3g, **Cholesterol** 55mg, **Sodium** 270mg, **Carbohydrates** 7g, **Dietary Fiber** 0g, **Protein** 22g
DIETARY EXCHANGES: ½ Bread/Starch, 3 Meat, ½ Fat

Chicken with Kale Stuffing

MAKES 4 SERVINGS

4 boneless skinless chicken breasts

1 cup sliced mushrooms

½ cup chopped onion

2 tablespoons dry white wine

1 teaspoon chopped fresh oregano *or* ¼ teaspoon dried oregano

1 clove garlic, minced

½ teaspoon black pepper

2 cups packed chopped stemmed kale

2 tablespoons light mayonnaise

½ cup seasoned dry bread crumbs

1. Pound chicken with meat mallet to ½-inch thickness; set aside.

2. Heat skillet over medium-high heat. Add mushrooms, onion, wine, oregano, garlic and pepper; cook and stir about 5 minutes or until onion is tender. Add kale; cook and stir until wilted.

3. Spread kale mixture evenly over flattened chicken breasts. Roll up chicken; secure with toothpicks. Brush chicken with mayonnaise; coat with bread crumbs.

4. Preheat air fryer to 370°F. Spray basket with nonstick cooking spray.

5. Cook chicken, seam sides down, 15 to 20 minutes or until chicken is golden brown and no longer pink in center. Remove toothpicks before serving.

Calories 240, **Total Fat** 6g, **Saturated Fat** 1g, **Cholesterol** 85mg, **Sodium** 200mg, **Carbohydrates** 14g, **Dietary Fiber** 1g, **Protein** 29g
DIETARY EXCHANGES: ½ Bread/Starch, 3½ Meat, ½ Vegetable, ½ Fat

Cauliflower Tacos
with Chipotle Crema

MAKES 8 TACOS

1 package (8 ounces) sliced cremini mushrooms

4 tablespoons olive oil, divided

¼ teaspoon salt

1 head cauliflower

1 teaspoon ground cumin

½ teaspoon dried oregano

¼ teaspoon ground coriander

¼ teaspoon ground cinnamon

¼ teaspoon black pepper

½ cup reduced-fat sour cream

2 teaspoons lime juice

½ teaspoon chipotle chili powder

½ cup vegetarian refried beans

8 (6-inch) corn or flour tortillas

Chopped fresh cilantro (optional)

Pickled Red Onions (recipe follows) or chopped red onion (optional)

1. Toss mushrooms with 1 tablespoon oil and salt in large bowl.

2. Remove leaves from cauliflower. Cut florets into 1-inch pieces; place in large bowl. Add remaining 3 tablespoons oil, cumin, oregano, coriander, cinnamon and black pepper; toss well.

3. Preheat air fryer to 390°F. Spray basket with nonstick cooking spray. Cook cauliflower 8 to 10 minutes or until browned and tender, shaking occasionally. Remove to large bowl.

4. Add mushrooms to basket. Cook 6 to 8 minutes or until browned, shaking occasionally.

5. For crema, combine sour cream, lime juice and chili powder in small bowl.

6. For each taco, spread 1 tablespoon beans and 1 teaspoon crema over each tortilla. Top with about 3 mushroom slices and ¼ cup cauliflower. Top with cilantro and red onions, if desired. Fold in half.

Pickled Red Onions: Thinly slice 1 small red onion; place in large glass jar. Add ¼ cup white wine vinegar or distilled white vinegar, 2 tablespoons water, 1 teaspoon sugar and 1 teaspoon salt. Seal jar; shake well. Refrigerate at least 1 hour or up to 1 week. Makes about ½ cup.

Calories 180, **Total Fat** 10g, **Saturated Fat** 2g, **Cholesterol** 10mg, **Sodium** 150mg, **Carbohydrates** 20g, **Dietary Fiber** 3g, **Protein** 5g
DIETARY EXCHANGES: 1 Bread/Starch, 1 Vegetable, 2 Fat

Balsamic Chicken

MAKES 6 SERVINGS

1½ teaspoons fresh rosemary leaves, minced, *or* ½ teaspoon dried rosemary

2 cloves garlic, minced

¾ teaspoon black pepper

½ teaspoon salt

6 boneless skinless chicken breasts (about ¼ pound each)

1 tablespoon olive oil

¼ cup balsamic vinegar

1. Combine rosemary, garlic, pepper and salt in small bowl; mix well. Place chicken in large bowl; drizzle chicken with oil and rub with spice mixture. Cover and refrigerate several hours.

2. Preheat air fryer to 390°F. Spray basket with nonstick cooking spray.

3. Cook in batches 10 to 12 minutes or until no longer pink in center. Remove to plates.

4. Drizzle vinegar over chicken.

Calories 170, **Total Fat** 5g, **Saturated Fat** 1g, **Cholesterol** 85mg, **Sodium** 250mg, **Carbohydrates** 2g, **Dietary Fiber** 0g, **Protein** 26g
DIETARY EXCHANGES: 3½ Meat, ½ Fat

Baked Catfish with Peach and Cucumber Salsa

MAKES 4 SERVINGS

¾ pound catfish fillet, rinsed and patted dry

½ teaspoon Italian seasoning

2½ tablespoons fresh bread crumbs

2 teaspoons unsalted butter, melted

½ cup peach or mango salsa

3 tablespoons coarsely chopped peeled cucumber

1. Preheat air fryer to 390°F. Line basket with parchment paper; spray with nonstick cooking spray.

2. Place fish in basket; sprinkle with Italian seasoning and bread crumbs; drizzle with butter. Cook 10 to 12 minutes, turning halfway through cooking, until fish begins to flake when tested with a fork.

3. Meanwhile, combine salsa and cucumber in small bowl; serve with fish.

Calories 160, **Total Fat** 7g, **Saturated Fat** 2.5g, **Cholesterol** 50mg, **Sodium** 210mg, **Carbohydrates** 9g, **Dietary Fiber** 0g, **Protein** 14g
DIETARY EXCHANGES: 2 Meat, 1 Vegetable, ½ Fat

Spicy Salmon

MAKES 4 SERVINGS

½ **teaspoon ground cumin**
½ **teaspoon chili powder**
¼ **teaspoon salt**
¼ **teaspoon black pepper**
¼ **teaspoon paprika**
4 **salmon fillets (about 4 ounces each)**

1. Combine cumin, chili powder, salt, pepper and paprika in small bowl. Rub over top of salmon.

2. Preheat air fryer to 350°F. Line basket with parchment paper; spray with nonstick cooking spray.

3. Cook 8 to 10 minutes or until salmon is lightly crispy and easily flakes when tested with a fork.

Serving Suggestion: Serve with tossed salad and rice.

Calories 240, **Total Fat** 15g, **Saturated Fat** 3.5g, **Cholesterol** 60mg, **Sodium** 220mg, **Carbohydrates** 0g, **Dietary Fiber** 0g, **Protein** 23g
DIETARY EXCHANGES: 3 Meat, 2 Fat

Baked Panko Chicken

MAKES 2 SERVINGS

½ cup panko bread crumbs

3 teaspoons assorted dried herbs (such as rosemary, basil, parsley, thyme or oregano), divided

Salt and black pepper

2 tablespoons mayonnaise

2 boneless skinless chicken breasts

1. Combine panko, 1 teaspoon herbs, salt and pepper in shallow dish. Combine mayonnaise and remaining 2 teaspoons herbs in small bowl. Spread mayonnaise mixture onto chicken. Coat chicken with panko mixture, pressing to adhere.

2. Preheat air fryer to 390°F. Line basket with parchment paper; spray with nonstick cooking spray.

3. Cook 18 to 20 minutes or until chicken is browned and no longer pink in center.

Calories 300, **Total Fat** 13g, **Saturated Fat** 2.5g, **Cholesterol** 90mg, **Sodium** 170mg, **Carbohydrates** 15g, **Dietary Fiber** 0g, **Protein** 28g
DIETARY EXCHANGES: 1 Bread/Starch, 3½ Meat, 2 Fat

Fish with Lemon Tarragon "Butter"

MAKES 2 SERVINGS

- **2 teaspoons margarine**
- **4 teaspoons lemon juice, divided**
- **½ teaspoon grated lemon peel**
- **¼ teaspoon mustard**
- **¼ teaspoon dried tarragon**
- **⅛ teaspoon salt**
- **2 lean white fish fillets (4 ounces each),* rinsed and patted dry**
- **¼ teaspoon paprika**

Cod, orange roughy, flounder, haddock, halibut and sole can be used.

1. Combine margarine, 2 teaspoons lemon juice, lemon peel, mustard, tarragon and salt in small bowl; mix well with a fork.

2. Preheat air fryer to 390°F. Spray basket with nonstick cooking spray. Drizzle fish with remaining 2 teaspoons lemon juice; sprinkle one side of each fillet with paprika.

3. Cook fish, paprika side down; 8 to 10 minutes until fish is opaque in center and begins to flake when tested with a fork. Top with margarine mixture.

Calories 120, **Total Fat** 4.5g, **Saturated Fat** 1g, **Cholesterol** 45mg, **Sodium** 250mg, **Carbohydrates** 1g, **Dietary Fiber** 0g, **Protein** 18g
DIETARY EXCHANGES: 2½ Meat, 1 Fat

Chicken Piccata

MAKES 4 SERVINGS

3 tablespoons all-purpose flour

½ teaspoon salt

¼ teaspoon black pepper

4 boneless skinless chicken breasts (4 ounces each)

1 teaspoon butter

2 cloves garlic, minced

¾ cup fat-free reduced-sodium chicken broth

1 tablespoon fresh lemon juice

2 tablespoons chopped fresh Italian parsley

1 tablespoon capers, drained

1. Combine flour, salt and pepper in shallow dish. Reserve 1 tablespoon flour mixture for sauce.

2. Pound chicken to ½-inch thickness between sheets of waxed paper with flat side of meat mallet or rolling pin. Coat chicken with remaining flour mixture, shaking off excess. Spray with nonstick cooking spray.

3. Preheat air fryer to 370°F. Line basket with parchment paper. Cook 15 to 20 minutes or until chicken is browned and no longer pink in center.

4. Heat butter and garlic in nonstick skillet over medium heat; cook and stir 1 minute. Add reserved flour mixture; cook and stir 1 minute. Add broth and lemon juice; cook 2 minutes or until sauce thickens, stirring frequently. Stir in parsley and capers; spoon sauce over chicken.

Calories 170, **Total Fat** 4g, **Saturated Fat** 1.5g, **Cholesterol** 85mg, **Sodium** 460mg, **Carbohydrates** 6g, **Dietary Fiber** 0g, **Protein** 27g
DIETARY EXCHANGES: ½ Bread/Starch, 3½ Meat

Dilled Salmon in Parchment

MAKES 2 SERVINGS

2   skinless salmon fillets
    (4 ounces each)
1   tablespoon butter, melted
1   tablespoon lemon juice
1   tablespoon chopped
    fresh dill
1   tablespoon chopped
    shallots
¼   teaspoon salt
⅛   teaspoon black pepper

1. Preheat air fryer to 370°F. Cut two pieces of parchment paper into 12-inch squares. Place fish fillets on parchment.

2. Combine butter and lemon juice in small bowl; drizzle over fish. Sprinkle with dill, shallots, salt and pepper. Wrap parchment around fish.

3. Cook 8 to 10 minutes or until fish is cooked through and easily flakes when tested with a fork.

Calories 290, **Total Fat** 21g, **Saturated Fat** 7g, **Cholesterol** 80mg, **Sodium** 360mg, **Carbohydrates** 1g, **Dietary Fiber** 0g, **Protein** 23g
DIETARY EXCHANGES: 3½ Meat, 3 Fat

Easy Air-Fried Chicken Thighs

MAKES 4 SERVINGS

8 bone-in or boneless chicken thighs with skin (about 1½ pounds)
½ teaspoon garlic powder
½ teaspoon onion powder
½ teaspoon dried oregano
½ teaspoon ground thyme
½ teaspoon paprika
¼ teaspoon salt
½ teaspoon black pepper

1. Place chicken in large resealable food storage bag. Combine garlic powder, onion powder, oregano, thyme, paprika, salt and pepper in small bowl; mix well. Add to chicken; shake until spices are distributed.

2. Preheat air fryer to 350°F. Line basket with parchment paper; spray with nonstick cooking spray.

3. Cook in batches 20 to 25 minutes until golden brown and cooked through, turning chicken halfway through cooking.

Calories 130, **Total Fat** 5g, **Saturated Fat** 1g, **Cholesterol** 95mg, **Sodium** 250mg, **Carbohydrates** 1g, **Dietary Fiber** 0g, **Protein** 20g
DIETARY EXCHANGES: 3 Meat

chapter 4

ON THE SIDE

Butternut Squash Fries

MAKES 4 SERVINGS

½ teaspoon garlic powder

¼ teaspoon salt

¼ teaspoon ground red pepper

1 butternut squash (about 2½ pounds), peeled, seeded and cut into 2-inch-thin slices

2 teaspoons vegetable oil

1. Combine garlic powder, salt and ground red pepper in small bowl; set aside.

2. Place squash in large bowl. Drizzle with oil and sprinkle with seasoning mix; gently toss to coat.

3. Preheat air fryer to 390°F. Cook in batches 16 to 18 minutes, shaking halfway during cooking, until squash is tender and begins to brown.

Calories 150, **Total Fat** 2.5g, **Saturated Fat** 0g, **Cholesterol** 0mg, **Sodium** 160mg, **Carbohydrates** 33g, **Dietary Fiber** 6g, **Protein** 3g
DIETARY EXCHANGES: 2 Bread/Starch, ½ Fat

Air-Fried Corn-on-the-Cob

MAKES 2 SERVINGS

2 teaspoons butter, melted

¼ teaspoon salt

½ teaspoon black pepper

½ teaspoon chopped fresh parsley

2 ears corn, husks and silks removed

Foil

Grated Parmesan cheese (optional)

1. Combine butter, salt, pepper and parsley in small bowl. Brush corn with butter mixture. Wrap each ear of corn in foil.*

2. Preheat air fryer to 390°F. Cook 10 to 12 minutes, turning halfway through cooking. Sprinkle with Parmesan cheese before serving, if desired.

*If your air fryer basket is on the smaller side, you may need to break ears of corn in half to fit.

Calories 110, **Total Fat** 5g, **Saturated Fat** 2.5g, **Cholesterol** 10mg, **Sodium** 310mg, **Carbohydrates** 17g, **Dietary Fiber** 3g, **Protein** 3g
DIETARY EXCHANGES: 1 Bread/Starch, ½ Fat

Kale Chips

MAKES 6 SERVINGS

1 large bunch kale (about 1 pound)
1 tablespoon olive oil
1 teaspoon garlic powder
½ teaspoon salt
½ teaspoon black pepper

1. Wash kale and pat dry with paper towels. Remove center ribs and stems; discard. Cut leaves into 2- to 3-inch-wide pieces.

2. Combine leaves, oil, garlic powder, salt and pepper in large bowl; toss to coat.

3. Preheat air fryer to 390°F.

4. Cook in batches 3 to 4 minutes or until edges are lightly browned and leaves are crisp. Cool completely. Store in airtight container.

Calories 60, **Total Fat** 3g, **Saturated Fat** 0g, **Cholesterol** 0mg, **Sodium** 230mg, **Carbohydrates** 7g, **Dietary Fiber** 3g, **Protein** 3g
DIETARY EXCHANGES: 1½ Vegetable, ½ Fat

Fried Cauliflower Florets

MAKES 4 SERVINGS

1 head cauliflower

1 tablespoon olive oil

3 tablespoons grated reduced-sodium Parmesan cheese

2 tablespoons panko bread crumbs

½ teaspoon salt

½ teaspoon chopped fresh parsley

¼ teaspoon ground black pepper

1. Cut cauliflower into florets. Place in large bowl. Drizzle with oil. Sprinkle Parmesan cheese, panko, salt, parsley and pepper over cauliflower; toss to coat.

2. Preheat air fryer to 390°F. Spray basket with nonstick cooking spray.

3. Cook in batches 18 to 20 minutes or until browned, shaking every 6 minutes during cooking.

Calories 100, **Total Fat** 5g, **Saturated Fat** 1.5g, **Cholesterol** 0mg, **Sodium** 350mg, **Carbohydrates** 10g, **Dietary Fiber** 3g, **Protein** 5g
DIETARY EXCHANGES: 1½ Vegetable, 1 Fat

Grilled Eggplant Roll-Ups

MAKES 2 SERVINGS

4 slices Grilled Eggplant (recipe follows)

¼ cup hummus

¼ cup crumbled reduced-fat feta cheese

¼ cup chopped green onions

4 tomato slices, cut in half

1. Prepare Grilled Eggplant. Spread 1 tablespoon hummus on each eggplant slice. Top with 1 tablespoon feta cheese, 1 tablespoon green onions and 2 tomato halves.

2. Roll up tightly. Serve immediately.

Grilled Eggplant: Preheat air fryer to 350°F. Spray basket with nonstick cooking spray. Sprinkle four (1-inch-thick) eggplant slices with ½ teaspoon salt; let stand 15 minutes. Spray eggplant with cooking spray. Cook in batches 5 minutes; turn and spray with cooking spray. Cook 5 minutes or until tender.

Calories 160, **Total Fat** 8g, **Saturated Fat** 3g, **Cholesterol** 10mg, **Sodium** 460mg, **Carbohydrates** 9g, **Dietary Fiber** 2g, **Protein** 8g
DIETARY EXCHANGES: 1 Meat, 1 Vegetable, 1 Fat

Savory Stuffed Tomatoes

MAKES 4 SERVINGS

2 large ripe tomatoes (1 to 1¼ pounds total)

¾ cup garlic- or Caesar-flavored croutons

¼ cup chopped pitted kalamata olives (optional)

2 tablespoons chopped fresh basil

1 clove garlic, minced

2 tablespoons grated Parmesan or Romano cheese

1 tablespoon olive oil

1. Cut tomatoes in half crosswise; discard seeds. Scrape out and reserve pulp. Set aside tomato shells.

2. Chop up tomato pulp; place in medium bowl. Add croutons, olives, if desired, basil and garlic; toss well. Spoon mixture into tomato shells. Sprinkle with cheese and drizzle oil over shells.

3. Preheat air fryer to 350°F. Line basket with foil or parchment paper.

4. Cook 5 to 7 minutes or until heated through.

Calories 100, **Total Fat** 7g, **Saturated Fat** 2g, **Cholesterol** 5mg, **Sodium** 270mg, **Carbohydrates** 8g, **Dietary Fiber** 1g, **Protein** 3g
DIETARY EXCHANGES: ½ Bread/Starch, ½ Vegetable, 1 Fat

Orange and Maple-Glazed Roasted Beets

MAKES 4 SERVINGS

4 medium beets, scrubbed

¼ cup orange juice

3 tablespoons balsamic or cider vinegar

2 tablespoons maple syrup

2 teaspoons grated orange peel, divided

1 teaspoon Dijon mustard

Salt and black pepper (optional)

1 to 2 tablespoons chopped fresh mint (optional)

1. Peel and cut beets in half lengthwise; cut into wedges. Place in large bowl.

2. Whisk orange juice, vinegar, maple syrup, 1 teaspoon orange peel and mustard in small bowl until well blended. Pour half over beets.

3. Preheat air fryer to 390°F.

4. Cook 22 to 25 minutes, shaking occasionally during cooking, until softened. Remove to serving dish; pour remaining orange juice mixture over beets. Season with salt and pepper. Sprinkle with remaining 1 teaspoon orange peel and mint, if desired.

Serving Suggestion: The flavors of this recipe make it a great side dish to serve at your holiday meal.

Calories 80, **Total Fat** 0g, **Saturated Fat** 0g, **Cholesterol** 0mg, **Sodium** 100mg, **Carbohydrates** 19g, **Dietary Fiber** 2g, **Protein** 2g
DIETARY EXCHANGES: 1½ Vegetable, ½ Other Carb

Baked Spinach Balls

MAKES 12 SERVINGS (2 PER SERVING)

1 package (6 ounces) sage and onion or herb-seasoned bread stuffing mix

1 small onion, chopped

2 tablespoons grated Parmesan cheese

1 clove garlic, minced

¼ teaspoon dried thyme

¼ teaspoon black pepper

1 package (10 ounces) frozen chopped spinach, thawed and well drained

¼ cup chicken broth

2 egg whites, beaten

Dijon or honey mustard (optional)

1. Combine stuffing mix, onion, cheese, garlic, thyme and pepper in medium bowl; mix well. Combine spinach, broth and egg whites in separate medium bowl; mix well. Stir into stuffing mixture. Cover; refrigerate 1 hour or until mixture is firm.

2. Preheat air fryer to 370°F.

3. Shape mixture into 24 balls. Cook in batches 5 minutes or until spinach balls are browned. Serve with mustard for dipping, if desired.

Calories 70, **Total Fat** 1g, **Saturated Fat** 0g, **Cholesterol** 0mg, **Sodium** 270mg, **Carbohydrates** 9g, **Dietary Fiber** 2g, **Protein** 4g
DIETARY EXCHANGES: ½ Bread/Starch, ½ Vegetable

Buffalo Cauliflower Bites

MAKES 4 SERVINGS

½ cup all-purpose flour

½ cup water

½ teaspoon garlic powder

¼ teaspoon black pepper

1 small head cauliflower, cut into small florets

3 tablespoons hot pepper sauce

1 tablespoon melted butter

Chopped fresh parsley

Blue cheese dressing and celery sticks

1. Preheat air fryer to 390°F. Line basket with parchment paper.

2. Combine flour, water, garlic powder and pepper in large bowl; stir until mixed. Add cauliflower; stir until florets are well coated.

3. Cook 12 to 15 minutes, shaking occasionally during cooking, until florets are slightly tender and browned.

4. Meanwhile, combine hot pepper sauce and butter in medium bowl. Add warm florets; toss well.

5. Sprinkle with parsley. Serve with blue cheese dressing and celery sticks.

Calories 80, **Total Fat** 0.5g, **Saturated Fat** 0g, **Cholesterol** 0mg, **Sodium** 400mg, **Carbohydrates** 16g, **Dietary Fiber** 2g, **Protein** 3g
DIETARY EXCHANGES: 1 Bread/Starch, ½ Vegetable

Orange Glazed Carrots

MAKES 6 SERVINGS

1 package (32 ounces) baby
  carrots
1 tablespoon packed light
  brown sugar
1 tablespoon orange juice
1 tablespoon melted butter
¼ teaspoon ground
  cinnamon
⅛ teaspoon ground nutmeg
  Orange peel and fresh
  chopped parsley
  (optional)

1. Place carrots in large bowl. Combine brown sugar, orange juice and butter in small bowl. Pour over carrots; toss well.

2. Preheat air fryer to 390°F.

3. Cook 6 to 8 minutes, shaking occasionally during cooking, until carrots are tender and lightly browned. Remove to serving dish. Sprinkle with cinnamon and nutmeg. Garnish with orange peel and parsley.

Calories 80, **Total Fat** 2g, **Saturated Fat** 1g, **Cholesterol** 5mg, **Sodium** 120mg, **Carbohydrates** 15g, **Dietary Fiber** 4g, **Protein** 1g
DIETARY EXCHANGES: 2½ Vegetable, ½ Fat

Potato Balls

MAKES 20 BALLS

- 2 cups refrigerated leftover mashed potatoes*
- 2 tablespoons all-purpose flour, plus additional for rolling balls
- ⅔ cup shredded reduced-fat Cheddar cheese
- ¼ cup chopped green onions
- 1 large egg
- ½ teaspoon salt
- ¼ teaspoon black pepper
- 1½ cups seasoned dry bread crumbs

*If you don't have leftover potatoes, prepare 2 cups instant mashed potatoes and refrigerate at least 1 hour.

1. Combine potatoes, 2 tablespoons flour, cheese and green onions in large bowl. Scoop out about 2 tablespoons mixture and roll into a 1-inch ball, adding additional flour, if necessary, making about 20 balls.

2. Beat egg, salt and pepper in medium bowl. Place bread crumbs in shallow dish. Dip balls in egg, then in bread crumbs until fully coated. Place on baking sheet; refrigerate 30 minutes.

3. Preheat air fryer to 390°F. Spray basket with nonstick cooking spray.

4. Cook in batches 8 to 10 minutes or until balls are browned and heated through.

Calories 70, **Total Fat** 1.5g, **Saturated Fat** 0.5g, **Cholesterol** 10mg, **Sodium** 270mg, **Carbohydrates** 12g, **Dietary Fiber** 0g, **Protein** 3g
DIETARY EXCHANGES: ½ Bread/Starch

chapter 5

SIMPLE STARTERS & SNACKS

Falafel Nuggets

MAKES 12 SERVINGS

Sauce

- 2½ cups tomato sauce
- ⅓ cup tomato paste
- 2 tablespoons lemon juice
- 2 teaspoons sugar
- 1 teaspoon onion powder
- ½ teaspoon salt

Falafel

- 2 cans (about 15 ounces each) chickpeas, rinsed and drained
- ½ cup all-purpose flour
- ½ cup chopped fresh parsley
- 1 egg
- ¼ cup minced onion
- 3 tablespoons lemon juice
- 2 tablespoons minced garlic
- 2 teaspoons ground cumin
- ½ teaspoon salt
- ½ teaspoon ground red pepper *or* red pepper flakes

1. For sauce, combine tomato sauce, tomato paste, 2 tablespoons lemon juice, sugar, onion powder and ½ teaspoon salt in medium saucepan. Simmer over medium-low heat 20 minutes or until heated through. Cover and keep warm until ready to serve.

2. For falafel, combine chickpeas, flour, parsley, egg, minced onion, 3 tablespoons lemon juice, garlic, cumin, ½ teaspoon salt and ground red pepper in food processor or blender; process until well blended. Shape mixture into 1-inch balls. Spray with nonstick cooking spray.

3. Preheat air fryer to 390°F. Line basket with foil; spray with cooking spray.

4. Cook in batches 12 to 15 minutes, turning halfway through cooking, until browned. Serve with sauce.

Calories 120, **Total Fat** 2g, **Saturated Fat** 0g, **Cholesterol** 15mg, **Sodium** 660mg, **Carbohydrates** 20g, **Dietary Fiber** 5g, **Protein** 6g
DIETARY EXCHANGES: 1 Bread/Starch, 1 Vegetable

Everything Seasoning Dip with Bagel Chips

MAKES ABOUT 2 CUPS DIP (16 SERVINGS)

2 large bagels, sliced vertically into rounds

1 container (12 ounces) whipped cream cheese

1½ tablespoons green onion tops, chopped

1 teaspoon minced onion

1 teaspoon minced garlic

1 teaspoon sesame seeds

1 teaspoon poppy seeds

¼ teaspoon kosher salt

1. Preheat air fryer to 350°F.

2. Coat bagel rounds generously with butter-flavored nonstick cooking spray. Cook 7 to 8 minutes or until golden brown, shaking occasionally.

3. Combine cream cheese, green onion, minced onion, garlic, sesame seeds, poppy seeds and salt in medium bowl; stir to blend.

4. Serve chips with dip.

Calories 110, **Total Fat** 8g, **Saturated Fat** 4.5g, **Cholesterol** 20mg, **Sodium** 170mg, **Carbohydrates** 8g, **Dietary Fiber** 0g, **Protein** 3g
DIETARY EXCHANGES: ½ Bread/Starch, 1½ Fat

Bite-You-Back Roasted Edamame

MAKES 4 SERVINGS

2 teaspoons vegetable oil

2 teaspoons honey

¼ teaspoon wasabi powder*

1 package (about 12 ounces) shelled edamame, thawed if frozen

Kosher salt (optional)

Wasabi powder can be found in the Asian section of most supermarkets and in Asian specialty markets.

1. Combine oil, honey and wasabi powder in large bowl; mix well. Add edamame; toss to coat.

2. Preheat air fryer to 370°F.

3. Cook 12 to 14 minutes, shaking occasionally during cooking, until lightly browned. Remove from basket to large bowl; sprinkle generously with salt, if desired. Cool completely before serving. Store in airtight container.

Calories 120, **Total Fat** 6g, **Saturated Fat** 0g, **Cholesterol** 0mg, **Sodium** 5mg, **Carbohydrates** 9g, **Dietary Fiber** 4g, **Protein** 10g
DIETARY EXCHANGES: ½ Bread/Starch, 1 Meat, ½ Fat

Turkey Meatballs with Yogurt-Cucumber Sauce

MAKES 30 MEATBALLS (6 SERVINGS)

1 pound lean ground turkey or chicken
1 cup finely chopped onion
½ cup plain dry bread crumbs
¼ cup whipping cream
2 cloves garlic, minced
1 egg, lightly beaten
3 tablespoons chopped fresh mint
1 teaspoon salt
¼ teaspoon ground red pepper
1 tablespoon olive oil
Yogurt-Cucumber Sauce (recipe follows)

1. Combine turkey, onion, bread crumbs, cream, garlic, egg, mint, salt and ground red pepper in large bowl; mix well. Shape into 30 meatballs. Place meatballs on baking sheet. Cover with plastic wrap; refrigerate 1 hour.

2. Preheat air fryer to 390°F. Line basket with parchment paper; spray with nonstick cooking spray.

3. Brush meatballs with oil. Cook in batches 12 to 14 minutes, shaking halfway through cooking, until cooked through.

4. Meanwhile, prepare Yogurt-Cucumber Sauce. Serve meatballs with sauce.

Yogurt-Cucumber Sauce

MAKES ABOUT 1 CUP

1 container (6 ounces) plain nonfat Greek yogurt
½ cup peeled seeded and finely chopped cucumber
2 teaspoons chopped fresh mint
2 teaspoons grated lemon peel
2 teaspoons lemon juice
¼ teaspoon salt

Combine all ingredients in small bowl. Refrigerate until ready to serve.

Calories 90, **Total Fat** 3.5g, **Saturated Fat** 1g, **Cholesterol** 35mg, **Sodium** 250mg, **Carbohydrates** 5g, **Dietary Fiber** 0g, **Protein** 12g
DIETARY EXCHANGES: 1½ Meat, ½ Fat

Spiced Sesame Wonton Crisps

MAKES 4 SERVINGS

1 tablespoon water

2 teaspoons olive oil

½ teaspoon paprika

½ teaspoon ground cumin or chili powder

¼ teaspoon dry mustard

10 (3-inch) wonton wrappers, cut into strips

Sesame seeds

1. Combine water, oil, paprika, cumin and mustard in small bowl; mix well.

2. Lightly brush wonton strips with oil mixture. Sprinkle with sesame seeds.

3. Preheat air fryer to 350°F. Spray basket with nonstick cooking spray.

4. Cook in single layer in batches 4 to 5 minutes or until browned and crunchy, shaking halfway through cooking. Remove to plate; cool completely.

Note: Your wonton crisps may curl up in the air fryer while cooking.

Calories 80, **Total Fat** 2.5g, **Saturated Fat** 0g, **Cholesterol** 0mg, **Sodium** 115mg, **Carbohydrates** 12g, **Dietary Fiber** 0g, **Protein** 2g
DIETARY EXCHANGES: 1 Bread/Starch, ½ Fat

Mini Pepper Nachos

MAKES 40 PEPPER HALVES (2 PER SERVING)

1 cup frozen corn, thawed

1 can (about 15 ounces) black beans, rinsed and drained

½ cup chopped tomatoes

½ teaspoon salt

20 mini sweet peppers, assorted colors, cut in half lengthwise and seeded

½ cup (2 ounces) shredded Mexican-style taco shredded cheese

½ cup sour cream (optional)

1 small avocado, chopped (optional)

2 tablespoons chopped green onion or cilantro (optional)

1. Combine corn, beans, tomatoes and salt in medium bowl. Fill peppers with about 1 tablespoon mixture. Sprinkle with cheese.

2. Preheat air fryer to 370°F. Line basket with foil. Cook peppers 5 to 7 minutes or until cheese is lightly browned and melted. Remove to serving plate.

3. Top with sour cream, avocado and green onion, if desired.

Calories 40, **Total Fat** 1g, **Saturated Fat** 0g, **Cholesterol** 5mg, **Sodium** 220mg, **Carbohydrates** 6g, **Dietary Fiber** 2g, **Protein** 2g
DIETARY EXCHANGES: ½ Bread/Starch

Great Zukes Pizza Bites

MAKES 8 SERVINGS (2 PER SERVING)

1 medium zucchini

3 tablespoons pizza sauce

2 tablespoons tomato paste

¼ teaspoon dried oregano

¾ cup (3 ounces) shredded part-skim mozzarella cheese

¼ cup shredded Parmesan cheese

8 slices pitted black olives

8 slices pepperoni (optional)

1. Preheat air fryer to 400°F; spray basket with nonstick cooking spray.

2. Trim off and discard ends of zucchini. Cut zucchini into 16 (¼-inch-thick) diagonal slices.

3. Combine pizza sauce, tomato paste and oregano in small bowl; mix well. Spread scant teaspoon sauce over each zucchini slice. Combine cheeses in small bowl. Top each zucchini slice with 1 tablespoon cheese mixture, pressing down into sauce. Place 1 olive slice on each of 8 pizza bites. Place 1 folded pepperoni slice on each remaining pizza bite, if desired.

4. Cook in batches 1 to 2 minutes or until cheese is melted. Serve immediately.

Calories 60, **Total Fat** 3.5g, **Saturated Fat** 1.5g, **Cholesterol** 10mg, **Sodium** 160mg, **Carbohydrates** 3g, **Dietary Fiber** 1g, **Protein** 4g
DIETARY EXCHANGES: ½ Meat, ½ Vegetable, ½ Fat

Roasted Chickpeas

MAKES 1 CUP (4 SERVINGS)

1 can (about 15 ounces)
  chickpeas, rinsed and
  drained
1 tablespoon olive oil
¼ teaspoon salt
¼ teaspoon black pepper
¼ tablespoon chili powder
¼ teaspoon ground red
  pepper
1 lime, cut into wedges
  (optional)

1. Combine chickpeas, oil, salt and black pepper in large bowl; toss to mix well.

2. Preheat air fryer to 390°F.

3. Cook 8 to 10 minutes, shaking occasionally during cooking, until chickpeas begin to brown.

4. Sprinkle with chili powder and ground red pepper. Serve with lime wedges, if desired.

Calories 120, **Total Fat** 4.5g, **Saturated Fat** 0g, **Cholesterol** 0mg, **Sodium** 390mg, **Carbohydrates** 15g, **Dietary Fiber** 4g, **Protein** 4g
DIETARY EXCHANGES: 1 Bread/Starch, ½ Fat

Mini Chickpea Cakes

MAKES 2 DOZEN CAKES (8 SERVINGS)

1 can (about 15 ounces) chickpeas, rinsed and drained

1 cup grated carrots

⅓ cup seasoned dry bread crumbs

¼ cup creamy Italian salad dressing, plus additional for dipping

1 egg

1. Coarsely mash chickpeas in medium bowl with fork or potato masher. Stir in carrots, bread crumbs, ¼ cup salad dressing and egg; mix well.

2. Shape chickpea mixture into 24 patties, using about 1 tablespoon mixture for each.

3. Preheat air fryer to 370°F. Spray basket with nonstick cooking spray.

4. Cook in batches 10 minutes, turning halfway through cooking, until lightly browned. Serve warm with additional salad dressing for dipping, if desired.

Calories 120, **Total Fat** 6g, **Saturated Fat** 1g, **Cholesterol** 25mg, **Sodium** 240mg, **Carbohydrates** 12g, **Dietary Fiber** 2g, **Protein** 4g
DIETARY EXCHANGES: ½ Bread/Starch, ½ Vegetable, 1 Fat

Cheesy Stuffed Mushrooms

MAKES ABOUT 18 MUSHROOMS

4   ounces Brie cheese, rind removed and cut into ½-inch cubes

8   ounces baby bella mushrooms, stems removed

½   cup seasoned dry bread crumbs

1   tablespoon fresh parsley leaves

2   tablespoons olive oil, divided

1. Insert cube of cheese inside each mushroom cap. Stir bread crumbs, parsley and 1 tablespoon oil in small dish. Top each mushroom with bread crumb mixture. Brush with remaining 1 tablespoon oil.

2. Preheat air fryer to 390°F.

3. Cook in batches 4 to 6 minutes or until topping is lightly browned.

Tip: Recipe can easily be doubled for a larger crowd.

Calories 50, **Total Fat** 3.5g, **Saturated Fat** 1.5g, **Cholesterol** 5mg, **Sodium** 85mg, **Carbohydrates** 3g, **Dietary Fiber** 0g, **Protein** 2g
DIETARY EXCHANGES: ½ Fat

Savory Pita Chips

MAKES 4 SERVINGS

2 whole wheat or white pita bread rounds

2 tablespoons grated Parmesan cheese

1 teaspoon dried basil

¼ teaspoon garlic powder

1. Carefully cut each pita round in half horizontally; split into two rounds. Cut each round into six wedges. Spray wedges with nonstick cooking spray.

2. Combine Parmesan cheese, basil and garlic powder in small bowl; sprinkle evenly over pita wedges.

3. Preheat air fryer to 350°F.

4. Cook 8 to 10 minutes, shaking occasionally during cooking, until golden brown. Cool completely.

Cinnamon Crisps: Substitute butter-flavored cooking spray for nonstick cooking spray and 1 tablespoon sugar mixed with ¼ teaspoon ground cinnamon for Parmesan cheese, basil and garlic powder.

Calories 100, **Total Fat** 1.5g, **Saturated Fat** 1g, **Cholesterol** 5mg, **Sodium** 230mg, **Carbohydrates** 18g, **Dietary Fiber** 0g, **Protein** 5g
DIETARY EXCHANGES: 1 Bread/Starch

Eggplant Nibbles

MAKES 4 SERVINGS

1 egg
1 tablespoon water
½ cup seasoned dry bread crumbs
1 Asian eggplant or 1 small globe eggplant
Marinara sauce (optional)

1. Beat egg and water in shallow dish. Place bread crumbs in another shallow dish.

2. Cut ends off of eggplant. Cut into sticks about 3 inches long by ½-inch wide.

3. Coat eggplant sticks in egg, then roll in bread crumbs. Spray with olive oil cooking spray.

4. Preheat air fryer to 370°F. Line basket with foil or parchment paper.

5. Cook 12 to 14 minutes, shaking occasionally during cooking, until eggplant is tender and lightly browned. Serve with marinara sauce, if desired.

Calories 100, **Total Fat** 2g, **Saturated Fat** 0.5g, **Cholesterol** 45mg, **Sodium** 220mg, **Carbohydrates** 17g, **Dietary Fiber** 3g, **Protein** 5g
DIETARY EXCHANGES: ½ Bread/Starch, 1½ Vegetable

chapter 6

DESSERT DELIGHTS

Yogurt Lime Tartlets

MAKES 8 TARTLETS

1 refrigerated pie crust (half of 15-ounce package)

1 cup plain nonfat Greek yogurt

2 tablespoons honey

1 egg, lightly beaten

Grated peel and juice of 1 lime

Additional grated lime peel (optional)

1. Unroll pie crust onto clean work surface. Cut out circles with 3-inch round cookie cutter. Re-roll scraps of dough to cut out total of eight circles. Press dough into bottoms and up sides of silicon muffin cups.

2. Stir yogurt, honey, egg, lime peel and lime juice in medium bowl until well blended. Spoon 1 tablespoon mixture into each muffin cup.

3. Preheat air fryer to 370°F. Cook 10 to 12 minutes or until filling is set and crust is golden brown. Cool 5 minutes. Remove to wire rack; cool completely. Refrigerate at least 2 hours before serving. Garnish with additional lime peel.

Calories 150, **Total Fat** 7g, **Saturated Fat** 3g, **Cholesterol** 30mg, **Sodium** 160mg, **Carbohydrates** 18g, **Dietary Fiber** 0g, **Protein** 5g
DIETARY EXCHANGES: 1 Bread/Starch, ½ Other Carb, 1 Fat

Sautéed Apples Supreme

MAKES 2 SERVINGS

2 small Granny Smith apples *or* 1 large Granny Smith apple

1 teaspoon butter, melted

2 tablespoons unsweetened apple juice or cider

1 teaspoon packed brown sugar

½ teaspoon ground cinnamon

⅔ cup vanilla ice cream or frozen yogurt (optional)

2 tablespoons chopped walnuts, toasted*

To toast nuts, cook in preheated 350°F parchment-lined air fryer 3 to 4 minutes or until golden brown.

1. Cut apples into quarters; remove cores and cut into ½-inch-thick slices. Toss butter and apples in medium bowl.

2. Combine apple juice, brown sugar and cinnamon in small bowl; toss with apples.

3. Preheat air fryer to 350°F. Line basket with parchment paper; spray with nonstick cooking spray.

4. Cook 6 to 8 minutes, shaking halfway through cooking, until soft and lightly golden. Transfer to serving bowls; serve with ice cream, if desired. Sprinkle with walnuts.

Calories 170, **Total Fat** 7g, **Saturated Fat** 1.5g, **Cholesterol** 5mg, **Sodium** 0mg, **Carbohydrates** 25g, **Dietary Fiber** 5g, **Protein** 2g
DIETARY EXCHANGES: 1½ Fruit, 1½ Fat

Chocolate Fruit Tarts

MAKES 6 TARTS

1 refrigerated pie crust (half of 15-ounce package)

1¼ cups prepared low-fat chocolate pudding (about 4 snack-size pudding cups)

1 cup fresh sliced strawberries, raspberries, blackberries or favorite fruit

1. Spray six (2½-inch) silicone muffin cups with nonstick cooking spray. Unfold pie crust on lightly-floured surface. Let stand at room temperature 15 minutes.

2. Roll out pie crust on clean work surface; cut out six circles with 4-inch round cookie cutter. Place dough circles in muffin cups, pleating around sides of cups. (Press firmly to hold dough in place.) Prick bottom and sides with fork.

3. Preheat air fryer to 370°F. Cook in batches 8 to 10 minutes or until golden brown. Carefully remove tart shells from muffin cups. Cool completely on wire rack.

4. Fill each tart shell with about 3 tablespoons pudding; arrange fruit on top.

Calories 210, **Total Fat** 9g, **Saturated Fat** 3.5g, **Cholesterol** 0mg, **Sodium** 220mg, **Carbohydrates** 31g, **Dietary Fiber** 1g, **Protein** 2g
DIETARY EXCHANGES: 1 Bread/Starch, ½ Other Carb, 1½ Fat

Peaches with Raspberry Sauce

MAKES 4 SERVINGS

1 package (10 ounces) frozen raspberries, thawed

1½ teaspoons lemon juice

2 tablespoons packed brown sugar

½ teaspoon ground cinnamon

1 can (15 ounces) peach halves in juice (4 halves)

Foil

2 teaspoons butter, cut into small pieces

Fresh mint sprigs (optional)

1. Combine raspberries and lemon juice in food processor fitted with metal blade; process until smooth. Refrigerate until ready to serve.

2. Preheat air fryer to 350°F.

3. Combine brown sugar and cinnamon in medium bowl; coat peach halves with mixture. Place peach halves, cut sides up, on foil. Dot with butter. Fold foil over peaches. Place packet in basket.

4. Cook 6 to 8 minutes or until peaches are soft and lightly browned.

5. To serve, spoon 2 tablespoons raspberry sauce over each peach half. Garnish with mint.

Calories 120, **Total Fat** 2g, **Saturated Fat** 1g, **Cholesterol** 5mg, **Sodium** 5mg, **Carbohydrates** 28g, **Dietary Fiber** 5g, **Protein** 1g
DIETARY EXCHANGES: 1½ Fruit, ½ Other Carb, ½ Fat

Upside-Down Apples

MAKES 2 SERVINGS

2 sheets heavy-duty foil

2 tablespoons finely chopped pecans or walnuts

2 tablespoons chopped dried apricots or any dried fruit

¼ teaspoon ground cinnamon

¼ teaspoon vanilla

⅛ teaspoon ground nutmeg

⅛ teaspoon salt

1 tablespoon honey or maple syrup

1 Fuji apple (about 8 ounces), halved and cored

½ cup vanilla ice cream (optional)

1. Spray foil with nonstick cooking spray.

2. Combine pecans, apricots, cinnamon, vanilla, nutmeg and salt in small bowl; mix well. Spread over foil. Drizzle with honey. Place apple halves on top of nut mixture, cut side down. Wrap foil around apple.

3. Preheat air fryer to 370°F. Cook 20 to 22 minutes or just until tender. Serve apple and nut mixture with ice cream, if desired.

Tip: Fuji apples are a combination of Red Delicious and Ralls Janet apples. They are crisp and juicy apples that hold their shape when baking. If Fuji apples are not available, substitute Braeburn or Gala apples.

Calories 180, **Total Fat** 5g, **Saturated Fat** 0g, **Cholesterol** 0mg, **Sodium** 150mg, **Carbohydrates** 34g, **Dietary Fiber** 4g, **Protein** 1g
DIETARY EXCHANGES: 1½ Fruit, ½ Other Carb, 1 Fat

Fried Pineapple with Toasted Coconut

MAKES 8 SERVINGS

1 large pineapple, cored and cut into chunks

½ cup packed brown sugar

1 teaspoon ground cinnamon

½ teaspoon ground nutmeg

½ cup toasted coconut*

Ice cream or whipped cream (optional)

Chopped macadamia nuts (optional)

Maraschino cherries (optional)

*To toast coconut in air fryer, place coconut in small ramekin. Cook in preheated air fryer at 350°F 2 to 3 minutes or until lightly browned.

1. Place pineapple chunks in large bowl. Combine brown sugar, cinnamon and nutmeg in small bowl; sprinkle over pineapple. Toss well. Refrigerate 30 minutes.

2. Preheat air fryer to 370°F. Spray basket with nonstick cooking spray.

3. Cook 6 to 8 minutes or until pineapple is browned and lightly crispy. Sprinkle with coconut. Serve with ice cream or macadamia nuts, if desired. Garnish with maraschino cherry.

Calories 140, **Total Fat** 2.5g, **Saturated Fat** 2g, **Cholesterol** 0mg, **Sodium** 5mg, **Carbohydrates** 31g, **Dietary Fiber** 2g, **Protein** 1g
DIETARY EXCHANGES: 1 Fruit, 1 Other Carb, ½ Fat

Baked Cinnamon Apples

MAKES 2 SERVINGS

2 large Granny Smith apples

2 sheets heavy-duty foil, lightly sprayed with nonstick cooking spray

2 tablespoons packed brown sugar

2 tablespoons dried cranberries

½ teaspoon ground cinnamon

2 teaspoons butter
Vanilla ice cream (optional)

1. Core apples. Using paring knife, trim off ½-inch strip around top of each apple. Place each apple in center of foil sheet.

2. Mix brown sugar, cranberries and cinnamon in small bowl. Fill inside of apples with sugar mixture, sprinkling any excess around pared rim. Place 1 teaspoon butter on sugar mixture on each apple; press gently.

3. Fold foil around apples.

4. Preheat air fryer to 350°F. Cook 12 to 14 minutes or until apples are slightly softened. Transfer apples to bowls; spoon remaining liquid over apples. Serve warm apples with ice cream, if desired.

Calories 240, **Total Fat** 4.5g, **Saturated Fat** 2.5g, **Cholesterol** 10mg, **Sodium** 5mg, **Carbohydrates** 50g, **Dietary Fiber** 7g, **Protein** 1g
DIETARY EXCHANGES: 2 Fruit, 1½ Other Carb, 1 Fat

Baked Pears

MAKES 4 SERVINGS

1 tablespoon sugar

¼ teaspoon ground cinnamon

2 medium ripe Bosc pears, halved lengthwise and cored

2 teaspoons butter

½ cup pear juice, divided

3 gingersnap cookies, crushed

1. Combine sugar and cinnamon in small bowl; sprinkle over pear halves. Put ½ teaspoon butter in each pear cavity. Drizzle 1 tablespoon juice over top of each pear.

2. Preheat air fryer to 370°F. Spray basket with nonstick cooking spray. Place pear halves, cut sides up, in basket.

3. Cook, cut-side up, 12 to 14 minutes or until pears are browned. Sprinkle with crushed gingersnaps; cook 3 to 4 minutes. Drizzle remaining ¼ cup juice over pears to serve.

Calories 200, **Total Fat** 4g, **Saturated Fat** 1.5g, **Cholesterol** 5mg, **Sodium** 115mg, **Carbohydrates** 40g, **Dietary Fiber** 3g, **Protein** 2g
DIETARY EXCHANGES: 1½ Fruit, ½ Fat

Index

Metric Conversion Chart

VOLUME MEASUREMENTS (dry)

¹/₈ teaspoon = 0.5 mL
¹/₄ teaspoon = 1 mL
¹/₂ teaspoon = 2 mL
³/₄ teaspoon = 4 mL
1 teaspoon = 5 mL
1 tablespoon = 15 mL
2 tablespoons = 30 mL
¹/₄ cup = 60 mL
¹/₃ cup = 75 mL
¹/₂ cup = 125 mL
²/₃ cup = 150 mL
³/₄ cup = 175 mL
1 cup = 250 mL
2 cups = 1 pint = 500 mL
3 cups = 750 mL
4 cups = 1 quart = 1 L

VOLUME MEASUREMENTS (fluid)

1 fluid ounce (2 tablespoons) = 30 mL
4 fluid ounces (¹/₂ cup) = 125 mL
8 fluid ounces (1 cup) = 250 mL
12 fluid ounces (1¹/₂ cups) = 375 mL
16 fluid ounces (2 cups) = 500 mL

WEIGHTS (mass)

¹/₂ ounce = 15 g
1 ounce = 30 g
3 ounces = 90 g
4 ounces = 120 g
8 ounces = 225 g
10 ounces = 285 g
12 ounces = 360 g
16 ounces = 1 pound = 450 g

DIMENSIONS

¹/₁₆ inch = 2 mm
¹/₈ inch = 3 mm
¹/₄ inch = 6 mm
¹/₂ inch = 1.5 cm
³/₄ inch = 2 cm
1 inch = 2.5 cm

OVEN TEMPERATURES

250°F = 120°C
275°F = 140°C
300°F = 150°C
325°F = 160°C
350°F = 180°C
375°F = 190°C
400°F = 200°C
425°F = 220°C
450°F = 230°C

BAKING PAN SIZES

Utensil	Size in Inches/Quarts	Metric Volume	Size in Centimeters
Baking or Cake Pan (square or rectangular)	8×8×2	2 L	20×20×5
	9×9×2	2.5 L	23×23×5
	12×8×2	3 L	30×20×5
	13×9×2	3.5 L	33×23×5
Loaf Pan	8×4×3	1.5 L	20×10×7
	9×5×3	2 L	23×13×7
Round Layer Cake Pan	8×1½	1.2 L	20×4
	9×1½	1.5 L	23×4
Pie Plate	8×1¼	750 mL	20×3
	9×1¼	1 L	23×3
Baking Dish or Casserole	1 quart	1 L	—
	1½ quart	1.5 L	—
	2 quart	2 L	—